Get a life!

Get a life!

A 5-session course
on calling
for young people

Tim Sledge
and Ally Barrett

A Youth Emmaus resource

CHURCH HOUSE
PUBLISHING

Church House Publishing
Church House
Great Smith Street
London SW1P 3AZ

Tel: 020 7898 1451
Fax: 020 7898 1449

ISBN 978 0 7151 4146 5

Published 2008 by Church House Publishing
Copyright © Tim Sledge and Ally Barrett 2008
Illustrations © Craig Cameron 2003, 2006

The opinions expressed in this book are those of the authors and do not necessarily reflect the official policy of the General Synod or The Archbishops' Council of the Church of England.

Printed in England by Halstan & Co Ltd, Amersham, Bucks

Contents

Acknowledgements

The authors would like to thank all the young people who have inspired them to compile this resource, as well as those who have helped to trial the sessions in one form or another, especially the Young Vocations Group in the Peterborough diocese, the youth group at St Mary's Church, Godmanchester, and Ely's *Rave in the Nave*.

Introduction

Jesus said: 'I came so that everyone would have life, and have it in its fullest.' *John 10.10 (CEV)*

Jesus said: 'Follow me . . . and I will send you out to fish for people.' *Mark 1.17 (CEV)*

Sometimes, people say to us that being a Christian must mean there are loads of things you can't do – implying that as soon as you become one or try to live a Christian life, things automatically become dull and dreary.

But as two Christians who are trying to live a Christian life, we want to say emphatically that this is not true! We worship a God who gave the life of his Son, and through our working and walking with Jesus we have gained a life, not lost one. Dull and dreary has become technicolor!

Of course it does not always feel that way, but following God has ultimately led us both into life! That's why those two Bible texts are such a strong motivation for us both.

What does it mean to be called to do something? How can we follow God's instincts for us rather than be influenced by peer pressure or be driven to wanting money and security and prosperity through other career paths? Indeed, if we are gifted in some of these areas, how can we serve God appropriately in them?

We long for this course to be an opportunity for young people to find out more about following Christ's call, which can happen in so many different ways. You don't need to be ordained to follow God's call, in fact most of you won't. For Jesus, being baptized was his response to God's call and his equipping through the Spirit into his ministry – tough, barren, isolating and yet utterly complete and full of joy. We pray that this small offering of a course might help the young people in the church and on the fringes of the church today to begin to look at what it means not just to follow Jesus but to respond to his calling and desire to give fulfilment in our lives.

Whether your young people become world leaders or sweep streets, are global economists or youth workers, we pray that they do it in response to God's call and find in turn abundance of life – that amazing vision of God's calling for each member of humanity.

Get a life!

Tim Sledge and Ally Barrett

Notes for leaders

What is it?

Get a life! is a 5-week course with an extra 'work shadow' session for young people aged 13 to18.

The aim of the course is to help young people realize that:

- they are called by God;

- through baptism and confirmation they are commissioned to serve God;

- calling and vocation can happen in many different ways, including vocation to lifelong Christian service;

- finding God's call for us is exciting and challenging!

Who is it for?

Get a life! is for young people aged 13 to 18, although the material would work with slightly younger or older people (even some adults!). It is for young people who have some level of spiritual maturity and enquiring minds. It is particularly useful as a post-confirmation course or for young people who at school or college are beginning to think about their options for GCSE or the direction of their life.

An ideal group size would be from 4 to 10 people.

How to run the course?

The course works well in a number of contexts:

- as a Lent course with an extra post-Easter session;

- as a 5-week course and 'work shadow';

- as a series of stand-alone sessions to be used in churches, schools or colleges;

- using some of the material, e.g. mega bytes, as part of Sunday morning nurture activities with young people;

- as a framework for a weekend away with young people.

What do the sessions consist of?

Each session is designed to last around 90 minutes and consists of:

home page

An outline of the sessions.

You will need:
a simple shopping list of materials and resources for the session.

interfacing

A prayer and reflection activity.

warming up

An icebreaker activity based on the theme of the session (up to 10 minutes).

backing up

A short summary of the ground you wanted to cover.

logging on

An outline of the session.

The handouts include:

byte

Short activities and reflections (about 15 minutes).

processing

Something to think about in the coming week.

mega byte

The key teaching aspect of each session (about 30 minutes).

do something about it

Ideas for practical involvement and 24/7 discipleship.

Who can lead this group?

We recommend two leaders for each group. The leaders do not have to be clergy, although, because of the nature of the material, you may find it useful to be able to call upon members of the church's ministry team or on a vocations adviser (or equivalent).

It is important that leaders don't come with all the answers but can journey alongside the young people as they share some deep things about their lives. The most important things are openness, honesty, deep value of and love for young people and a willingness to be vulnerable as an adult too.

It is important that the leaders are open to God and willing to continue to be moulded by God's grace and calling on their lives. None of us has fully 'arrived' as a Christian or has all the answers, but we need to be confident and rooted in prayer and the Scriptures to facilitate the groups as well as possible.

Make sure you are well prepared

Read the notes and the *You will need* section carefully and thoroughly. *Get a life!* relies on human resources and guest speakers and people who are willing to share of themselves and their time. You will need to invite them in good time and brief them well.

Please do serve good refreshments in a pleasant environment. Young people are worth it! One way to show this is to provide quality refreshments before, during or after the session – whatever works best for you. We believe that hospitality is a God-given gift and speaks volumes about our commitment to young people in your church, school or college.

For some of the sessions you will need some space and a DVD player. We recommend meeting in comfortable surroundings with comfy chairs or big cushions so that the group can sit in a circle.

Child protection

The welfare of young people and their leaders is paramount. Each church or organization will have its own child protection policy, which needs to be strictly adhered to.

If you are in any doubt, please contact the person in your church who is responsible for child protection and for group insurance for young people. If you are still unclear, contact your denominational child protection policy adviser. All adults working with (and visiting) the groups need to have undertaken a Criminal Records Bureau (CRB) check.

Establishing the ground rules

We suggest using part of the initial meeting to help to create an environment of trust, openness and respect. So suggest and/or get the young people to set up some ground rules for your meeting. These might vary from not talking when others are talking to not laughing at others' suggestions, or not talking outside the room about what people have said. You could have a slogan: 'Less gossip, more generosity' or 'Less "am I bovvered?", more "I am bothered"'.

Getting the whole church on board

It has been a long and fruitful tradition of the Church to pray for vocations, which has focused historically on the desire for more people to come forward to be priests and ministers. Running this course would be a really good time to extend the scope of this prayer, praying specifically for young people, that they might hear, understand and be faithful to the calling that God may be placing on their lives to use their gifts for building the kingdom of God, as they seek to serve God in voluntary work, specific paid work or their chosen career. There are plenty of stockbrokers, doctors, teachers, window cleaners and care workers who are fulfilling God's call on their lives.

You might want to use this prayer both in corporate worship and for individual use for the rest of the church as the course is running:

> **Loving God, in baptism you called us into life.**
>
> **We thank you for the gift of life and the gifts you have given in our lives.**
>
> **We pray particularly for our young people,**
>
> **that guided by you and supported by your Church,**
>
> **they may seek your purposes in their lives,**
>
> **find perfect freedom in your service,**
>
> **and reveal your glory in the world.**
>
> **We ask this through Christ our Lord. Amen.**

Bible versions

Bible quotations are taken from the Today's New International Version (TNIV) and the Contemporary English Version (CEV), but this does not preclude the use of other versions. Many of these are available on **www.biblegateway.com**.

Taking young people seriously

Young people are constantly asked what they want to do when they grow up, but the question is rarely asked in a Christian context. Year 11, year 13, and after further and higher education courses are particular times when young people are thinking about what to do next, and about what their future career might be, and starting to question their own identity and where they are going in life.

Young people are often under a great deal of stress from exams and coursework deadlines, along with peer pressure to conform to (often unhealthy) behaviour patterns. While it can be helpful to explore together the factors that affect young people's options when it comes to employment and careers, it can be very countercultural to profess faith in this context, much less talk about a sense of calling from God.

Young people and children are often not taken seriously either in society generally or in the Church. In the community, young people are often perceived as a problem to be dealt with, or resented, and in church, they may be valued (if they are valued at all) as 'the Church of the future' rather than as the Church of the present. So it's always worth asking how young people might gain a higher profile and how their gifts might be exercised more fully in the contexts in which they find themselves. For example, in church, this might mean acting as sidespersons/welcomers, servers, readers, intercessors; presenting drama; giving testimony; involvement with healing ministry; or in leadership role within their youth group. There will be other ways for young people to have a higher profile within their own networks and in the wider community.

It hardly needs saying, but Christian young people are of equal value to adult Christians by virtue of their baptism. Indeed, God always has spoken to children and young people (cf 1 Samuel 3), and still does today. The Church and society in general have much to gain from all they have to offer. Even more important is that we are all of equal value through our shared humanity.

Role modelling

Role models are hugely important for young people, and it will be helpful if the youth leaders and other adults they encounter can provide a realistic model for discipleship, ministry and service.

Most young people are encouraged or required by their school or college to undertake at least one period of work experience or work shadowing. As part of *Get a life!*, all members of the group are asked to undertake a short work-shadowing placement (perhaps half a day or even just a couple of hours) and/or an interview with a Christian in secular employment or perhaps with someone involved in ministry (see Session 4a). Resource sheet 1 can be given to those offering placements. Resource sheet 2 is for the young people to help them get the most out of the experience.

It would also be worth talking to a local school or college, to offer a work experience placement based at the church, or with a member of the ministry team who feels confident about supervising a young person (provided that appropriate child protection rules can be maintained, and within pastorally appropriate limits). This needs careful forethought, but can be immensely worthwhile not only for what the young people can learn, but also for what they can teach the ministers.

Youth leaders can help by being honest about their personal experience of calling and ministry (both as a youth leader, and in other aspects of their lives), always reiterating that each person's experience is different.

Be prepared to point members of your group to where they can find information on further opportunities for exploring their vocations, such as gap year projects, voluntary work, careers fairs, Greenbelt (see below).

Information on ordained, licensed or authorized Christian ministry will be available through your church; each denomination has its own structures, and your clergy or minister will know how to tap into these.

A small sample of Christian organizations is listed below:

Careforce seeks to serve evangelical churches and organizations by placing Christian volunteers aged 17 to 30 where help is most needed in the UK, and to enable Christians from the UK and other countries worldwide to serve for a year in the UK in an area of need alongside local Christians: **www.careforce.co.uk**

Christian Aid also offers gap year projects, working in the UK with other young people in campaigning, fund-raising and event management:
www.pressureworks.org.uk/dosomething/Gap/index.html

Church of England Ministry Division has a section on its web site devoted to encouraging vocations for young people to ordained ministry. Your local diocesan director of ordinands will be able to help you more or visit
www.cofe.anglican.org/lifeevents/ministry/ministryinthecofe/ for more details.

L'Arche welcomes applications to participate in its communities of adults (both with and without intellectual disabilities). There are nine communities in the UK and many more in over 30 countries worldwide: **www.larche.org**

Ridley Hall Centre for Youth Ministry
The Centre for Youth Ministry (CYM) offers the chance to study at Ridley Hall for an honours degree in Youth and Community Work and Applied Theology. It is a unique vocational course giving the opportunity to study for a theology degree and receive the professional JNC youth workers' qualification. The professional qualification is a licence to practise and the gateway to an exciting and varied career in youth and community work: **www.ridley.cam.ac.uk/contactcym.html**

Scripture Union's 'Action Now' project offers tailor-made work experience placements (anything up to a whole year) for school leavers, with their nationwide team of workers: **www.scriptureunion.org.uk**.

Xplore is a new Church Army global gap year scheme: **www.xploreglobal.org.uk**

www.greenbelt.org.uk – for details of different ways to explore voluntary work and a variety of vocational avenues.

Youth for Christ is able to offer advice on Christian gap year projects and opportunities, particularly overseas: **www.yfc.co.uk**

www.christiangapyear.org.uk is a useful source of other ideas.

gifts: have you got the x-factor?

home page

This session starts by asking each of us to look at our own gifts and talents, how we use them (or abuse them) and where they fit into our relationship with God and with each other.

You will need:

* some small pieces of paper or card headed 'gift token', some pens and an attractive lidded box (the 'gift box') – a local craft shop or 'scrapstore' (see **www.childrensscrapstore.co.uk**) will be able to help you with many of these materials;
* a tennis ball or small sponge ball;
* a large sheet of paper (big enough to draw round someone);
* smaller pieces of paper, sticky tape and pens;
* items for the 'buried treasure' exercise, hidden before the session begins;
* coins for the acted-out parable;
* a flip chart and marker pens (for each session, to jot down discussion points).

warming up

Get everyone to introduce themselves, by saying their name and something they are good at. Alternatively, invite each person to act out the gift they feel they have, as in the game 'charades'.

Then, to make it more lively, try throwing a ball to each other and saying the name and talent of the person to whom you're throwing.

If you want to set some ground rules for the group (see Introduction notes), you could play the same game and suggest rules as you throw the ball to each other.

logging on

Explain that this course is about how God calls us in every aspect of our lives – he is interested in the whole of us, not just when we are in church or at youth group. It is also about how we can live fruitfully – enjoying life in all its fullness – by hearing God's call and following his way. It is about listening to God's promptings whenever we make decisions about the way we live – the big, life-changing decisions such as what jobs or courses we will apply for, and also the hundreds of small decisions we make every day.

continued >

gifts: have you got the x-factor?

logging on

continued >

Talk about the need to find a role model (a Christian engaged in a Christian or secular job) with whom they would undertake a half-day of work shadowing, and conduct an interview. Invite them to keep a journal during the course, in which they can note down things they want to remember, especially things that they have found encouraging, interesting, or challenging.

Then explain that this session is about gifts. Each of us has different gifts and abilities that God has given to us to make the most of for our own personal development, in the service of others, and in God's service. No two people have exactly the same set of gifts, and everyone's gifts are important and valuable.

byte

Body building

On the large sheet of paper, draw round one of the members of the group, then read 1 Corinthians 12.14-30, introducing the idea of the Church, and indeed, society, as a 'body' in which everyone has an important function.

Ask all present to write their name or initials on the body part where they think they have a gift (e.g. a good listener might write on the ears, and a footballer on the feet).

- Where do we see ourselves in this body?

- What body parts are over-represented?

- What body parts are overlooked or missing?

- In the body of the Church or of society in general, who is generally overlooked? What do they offer to the body as a whole?

- Who does all the bits that nobody else wants to do?

gifts: have you got the x-factor?

byte

With compliments

This exercise works best when the members of the group know each other well. Tape a piece of paper to each person's back, and give every member of the group a pen. Ask them to circulate around the room, writing down something that they admire about each other on that person's piece of paper. Everyone should end up with a list of their own gifts and talents – what makes them special.

Then ask the group:

● How easy was it to spot the good things about other people?

● Were there any surprises in your own list?

Make the point that sometimes we are good at knocking people and not so good at building them up. Get them to think for a moment about the last time they paid someone – anyone – a compliment or said something good about someone instead of saying something bad.

byte

Buried treasure

Hide in the meeting room beforehand a series of symbols representing gifts that aren't always recognized or celebrated, or that are ambiguous, such as:

● A pair of headphones (listening). *A 'quiet' gift that can make a big difference to people – often it helps more to be listened to attentively than to have someone jump in and try to 'fix' your problem;*

● A briefcase/laptop (good head for business, entrepreneurship, or drive to succeed). *How does the group feel about those who are gifted in the world of commerce – is it something to be admired and desired, or something that feels somehow 'ungodly'? Does God call people to work in business and commerce?*

● A red pen (the ability to give criticism). *Think about how much difference it makes when you receive good constructive criticism rather than meaningless praise or comments that undermine. How hard is it to give useful criticism? Do you know anyone who is gifted in this way?*

continued >

gifts: have you got the x-factor?

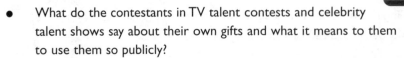

byte

continued >

- A fairtrade energy bar or some organic fairtrade fruit (looking after ourselves). *How important it is to look after our bodies, and to eat well with concern for the environment and for those who produce our food.*

- Others that you might have available, e.g. stethoscope (doctors and healing profession), oven gloves (catering and school dinners), nappy (mothers and carers).

Hunt for these gift symbols and then invite the group to think about how we can recognize more unusual or 'difficult' gifts in ourselves and in others? Why are some gifts hard to find in ourselves or in others?

Are there other examples of difficult gifts?

mega byte

If you've got it, flaunt it!

Ask the group:

- If each member of the group had to enter a talent contest, what would they choose to do?

- What do the contestants in TV talent contests and celebrity talent shows say about their own gifts and what it means to them to use them so publicly?

Then read, mime with a narrator, or act out, the Parable of the Talents (Matthew 25.14-30).

Ask the group:

- What are the benefits of using our gifts?

- What are the risks to using our gifts?

- Is it possible to misuse our gifts?

- What might stop us using our gifts?

- What happens when people don't use their gifts?

- How can we get better at seeing where our gifts might be used for our own enjoyment, in the service of others and in the service of God?

gifts: have you got the x-factor?

byte

Take it back to the shop!

Ask each person in the group to think of a time when they were given a gift with which they were disappointed. Why was the gift inappropriate? Is there any way that the gift could have been 'redeemed', or was it really useless? Some examples might include:

- A hairslide given to someone with very short hair – could be kept in case you grow your hair, or given away.

- A pair of socks – is always useful, even if it's not all that interesting.

- A musical instrument given to someone who doesn't know how to play it – might inspire them to learn something new.

Can the group think of examples of a talent that might be unwanted or unwelcome? Does anyone in the group have any experience of being good at something they're not interested in, or having a gift that they find difficult, such as a serious talent for tennis in someone who has always wanted to be a footballer, or someone who is bilingual always being asked to translate for everyone else.

How do they deal with it?

How can we play to our strengths and make the most of what seems like a 'pointless' gift?

How might those unwanted gifts turn out to be useful or fruitful?

interfacing

Gift tokens

Place all the items used during today's session in the centre of the room, and arrange the chairs in a circle. Take a moment of quiet to remember what you have discussed today.

Place the 'gift box' in the middle on a small table, and give out the 'gift tokens' and pens. Invite all the members of the group to write on their own gift token a talent or ability they believe they have (this is God's gift to each of us) and to come forward and place it in the gift box (that is our gift back to God as we offer all that we can do in his service).

After a moment of quiet, thank God for the gifts that each person brings. Ask for his grace in finding them and using them.

Finish with the prayer on the handout.

backing up

We all have something to offer to God, and to each other. All our gifts are valuable in the service of God.

gifts: have you got the x-factor?

home page

Even if we don't realize it, we each have gifts and talents; the question is how we use them (or mis-use them) and where they fit into our relationship with God and with each other.

byte

Body building

How do you fit in — where are you on the body?

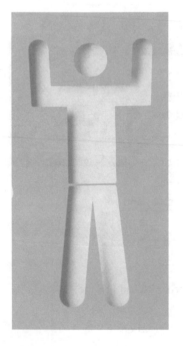

byte

With compliments

Write down

Things I knew about myself

....

....

....

....

Things that only other people seemed to know about me

....

....

....

>

gifts: have you got the x-factor?

mega byte

If you've got it, flaunt it!

Parable of the Talents (Matthew 25.14-30).

- How do the people in the parable of the talents feel?
- How do you feel about what you have been given?
- What are the risks?
- What are the joys?
- What happens if we do nothing?

byte

Buried treasure

What are the 'difficult' gifts?

byte

Take it back to the shop!

How can we make the most of a gift we don't want?

interfacing

Gift tokens

Lord, you made us all unique, with so much to offer, and so much to enjoy.

Thank you for all that you have given to us.

Accept what we offer you now through Jesus Christ our Lord. Amen.

processing

- What did you offer to God today?
- Has it made you feel differently about your abilities and talents?
- Have you learned something new about yourself? Or about someone else?

do something about it

How will offering your gifts to God affect you in the next week?

Think of some practical ways to 'contribute to the body', especially if it means using a gift you didn't know you had!

vocation: it's your call

You will need:

* flip chart and pens;
* chairs, or other obstacles, and a scarf to use as a blindfold;
* sheets of paper and pictures from Supplementary resources sheet 2 for 'Go with your passions' exercise.

home page

Vocation is a word often used for those in the caring professions, or even just about those in ordained ministry or religious life. But literally it means 'calling', and God calls us in many different ways and in every aspect of our lives. The idea that God might speak to us can be unnerving, and it's often not clear what we mean by God 'speaking'. This session explores how we hear the call of God and what God might be saying to us.

warming up

Simon says

Play the game of *Simon says*, first in the usual way, with the leader giving instructions and obeying the instructions themselves (e.g. 'Simon says "put your hands on your head"' and the leader doing the action for everyone to copy).

Then play it slightly differently with the leader giving out one instruction but miming something different (e.g. 'Simon says "put your hands on your head"' and the leader clasps his or her hands together instead). The first time, they should try to obey the spoken instruction, and the second time they should try to follow the action and ignore the words. Still include the usual trick of giving some instructions without saying 'Simon says' at all!

This game is harder than it looks – it is hard to work out what to do when there are contradictory signals being given out!

logging on

God calls everyone by name, from before we are born, and at our baptism/confirmation, and in fact, every day of our lives! But how does God communicate with us, and what might God be saying to us?

byte

Follow me!

Blindfold a volunteer from the group, and then set up an obstacle course of chairs, etc.

Ask the volunteer to nominate someone they trust to help them navigate a route through the room by giving verbal instructions only. Then do it again with other members of the group shouting out unhelpful directions. Finally, do it again with the 'guide' gently nudging the volunteer in the right direction while the group continues to shout out unhelpful instructions.

Ask the volunteer about the experience.

● How hard or easy was it to hear the voice they were supposed to be following?

● What was it like to trust one voice and ignore the others?

● Was it easier to follow what was said, or the guidance given by touch?

Widen the discussion to the whole group, and reflect:

● If God is the one we trust, how do we recognize his voice?

By experience – he has led us faithfully in the past?

By what he says – that he doesn't lead us into danger?

By the way he says it – God invites us, rather than bullies us?

● What might the other 'voices' be, in real life?

Peer pressure, advertising, etc.

Expectations and tradition.

Temptation and negative influences.

Pride, arrogance, wanting to do things our own way.

vocation: it's your call

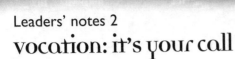

A call from God isn't usually like hearing a voice. More often it comes through our gifts (as we spoke of in the previous session) and also through our passions – what really 'fires us up'. Jesus said 'Where your treasure is, there is your heart also.' Our passions are gifts from God, and where we feel most strongly, either positively or negatively, is often the place where God speaks to us. For example, Live8 came about because of Bono and Bob Geldof's passion for the poor. Their anger has led to huge amounts of money being raised. Desmond Tutu was passionate about ending apartheid and his passion has contributed to reconciliation in South Africa.

So where are your passions? What fires you up? What makes you angry and what gives you a 'tingle factor' of excitement?

Cut out the pictures of different-sized hearts (positive passions) and screams (righteous anger) on Supplementary resources sheet 2, and have these in the centre of the room with some sticky tack.

Then write or print the following words on pieces of A4 paper and stick them around the room and invite the group to stick either a heart or a scream on the word to indicate what passion this evokes.

(The following are just suggestions; you might want to have a brainstorm with the group about people's current passions and angers and add their suggestions on some spare blank sheets of paper.)

Food	Bullying
Love	College place
Money	Politics
Success	Litter
Poverty	Binge drinking
Racism	Sex

If you wanted to make it more fun, suggest that, as they stick their scream or heart they make an appropriate noise at a volume to indicate their passion or anger!

vocation: it's your call

mega byte

It's your call

Read or act out either:

- the story of the boy Samuel in the Temple (1 Samuel 3.1-10), or

- the story of Elijah hiding in the cleft of the rock (1 Kings 19.9-13, adding some context from the rest of the chapter).

If you have plenty of time, it would be good to use both stories.

Based on the experience of Elijah and/or Samuel, ask the group:

- Who helps us hear the call of God (Samuel story)? It can be helpful to bounce ideas off other people if we think God might be leading us in a particular direction.

- In what situations are we most likely to be able to hear God (both stories)?

- What stops us hearing the call of God (both stories)?

- What is the call of God like (both stories)?

- Whom does God call (Samuel story)? Often it is those who are overlooked.

- Does God tell us exactly what we always expect or hope to hear (both stories)?

- Is the voice of God what we expect (Elijah story)?

- Have you ever felt that God has spoken to you – maybe even at baptism or confirmation (by our names)? Would any of the group be willing to share their experience? Remember that God 'speaks' not just in words, but in all sorts of other ways, too.

byte

One-2-one

Look at the quotations on the supplementary handout.

How does it feel that God might speak to you personally?

- Amazing?

- Unlikely?

- Scary?

vocation: it's your call

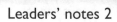

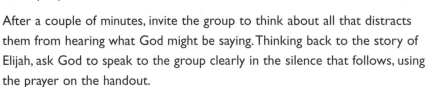

interfacing

The sound of silence

Spend some time as a group in silence with eyes closed. To many people, silence can be a bit intimidating, so just ask the group to get comfy, lie on the floor or in a relaxed position and to breathe in and out slowly. Encourage the group to notice all the sounds they are hearing around them, such as cars, nature, other people.

After a couple of minutes, invite the group to think about all that distracts them from hearing what God might be saying. Thinking back to the story of Elijah, ask God to speak to the group clearly in the silence that follows, using the prayer on the handout.

After another few moments of quiet, invite the group to offer (silently) to God all that they found themselves thinking about, and perhaps to jot down some thoughts on the handout.

backing up

God can speak to us in so many different ways, including:

- the Bible;

- opportunities or challenges we face;

- gifts, skills, and talents;

- passions and enthusiasms;

- prayer;

- other people (friends, leaders);

- ideas that we think are our own;

- coincidences/'Godincidences'.

If we are ready to listen, we will hear him.

vocation: it's your call

home page

'Vocation' is often used about those in the caring professions or religious life. But literally it means 'calling', and Christians believe that God calls us in many different ways and in every aspect of our lives. The idea that God might speak to us can be unnerving, and it's often not clear what we mean by God 'speaking'. How can we hear the call of God and what God might be saying to us today?

byte

Follow me!

What are the voices that distract you from listening to God?

What sorts of decision do they affect?

How easy or hard is it to hear the voice of God amid all the other voices?

byte

Go with your passions

What makes you angry? What concerns you?

What gets you excited and gives you a bit of the 'tingle' factor?

mega byte

It's your call

Who or what can help us hear God?

In what situations are we likely to hear God?

What sorts of thing does God say?

What is the voice of God like?

Have you ever felt that God was speaking to you?

vocation: it's your call

byte

One-2-one

What if God spoke to you personally?

interfacing

The sound of silence

Lord,
Speak to us
in the stillness,
and help us to hear your call.
Amen.

processing

In what situations do you best hear the voice of God? Who or what might be able to help you?

Did you feel that God was saying anything to you today?

do something about it

Try to be aware of how conflicting pressures (from TV advertising, peer pressure, your own and other people's expectations) affect your decision-making. Consider how God might speak to you through these things.

Then perhaps try an evening without television/radio, phone, texting, or the Internet: find some time to be still, asking God to speak to you in the silence. If you find it hard to spend time in silence, you could try:

- making sure you are somewhere you won't be disturbed, and that you are comfortable, perhaps sitting on a floor cushion with your back to a wall, or even lying down;

- closing your eyes, or focusing your attention on something like a candle flame (being careful, of course!) or a simple calming picture (such as a poster of a sunset or tranquil landscape);

- folding your hands, or placing them in your lap, or perhaps even holding something like a 'holding cross';

- slowing your breathing down, and tensing then relaxing each muscle in turn, starting with your toes and working upwards;

- setting yourself just a short time of quiet to begin with, until you get used to the feeling of being still – you may find you get to like it!

vocation: it's your call

I'd no idea what I really wanted to do with my life, but then someone suggested that I should be a teacher – I don't know how they knew that it would be the right thing for me, but it is.

A trainee teacher

From a position of gratitude for what Jesus had done for me (and you), I wanted to make sure that I was doing what he wanted me to do with my life. So I asked him.

An ordinand

I'd always felt that there was something I should be doing with my life, but I didn't know what it was. So when I felt that God was calling me, it was still surprising, but it felt like I was recognizing something I already really knew.

A youth worker

Isn't it true, though, that God only needs to really shout (like by appearing in a burning bush or by sending thunderbolts) when people aren't listening properly in the first place?

A teenager

I'm not the sort of person who hears voices or has spiritual experiences, but when I sat down and looked at my life, it seemed as if God had arranged everything in order to point me in a certain direction, and that I should simply try following it to see where it led.

An overseas development worker

I started a degree in dentistry partly because my parents wanted me to train for something that would be useful, and that would result in my actually getting a job when I graduated, but the more I thought about it, the more I realized that in my own small way I could make a real difference to people doing this. It made sense, and maybe it really is what I'm supposed to be doing.

A trainee dentist

I didn't hear any words, but it was as if God spoke directly into my heart.

A first experience of God's call

Believe it or not, I used to be a personnel officer for a big company. It was OK, and I had enough spare time to do what I really love – the children's magic shows and the ventriloquism and all that. But then, when I was made redundant, I started to wonder whether this was God telling me that I should take a good look at my life, and maybe that what had been a hobby might actually earn me a living – my life is totally different now, and I've never looked back.

An entertainer

The call seemed to come out of the blue, and turned my whole world upside down. But eventually I began to question whether it had even been the right way up in the first place.

A monk

vocation: it's your call

Hearts and screams images for 'Go with your passions'

ministries: working them out!

home page

To think about what it means to live out God's calling in our everyday lives and in our work.

warming up

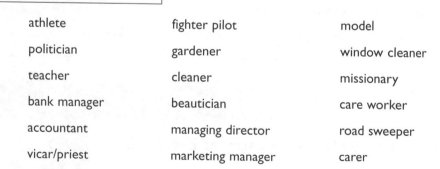

Fab, sad, mad or bad!

This is a game where people have to vote on jobs and what they think of them:

Place the four large pieces of paper with one of the words fab, sad, mad or bad in four corners or spaces in the room. Everyone in the group needs to stand in the centre of the room and, as you read out these jobs and occupations, they have to run to what they think is the image of this work:

athlete	fighter pilot	model
politician	gardener	window cleaner
teacher	cleaner	missionary
bank manager	beautician	care worker
accountant	managing director	road sweeper
vicar/priest	marketing manager	carer

Of all these, which is attractive? Which ones do you know about? Which ones do you know nothing about?

How can each of them be seen not just as jobs, but as ministries?

Can the group think of any examples of Christian sportsmen, politicians, etc? How has their faith made a difference to their work?

ministries: working them out!

byte

What is a ministry?

Minister is defined in a dictionary as a verb and means 'to serve, to attend to the needs of, to help'.

Play a quick word association game: when the leader says 'minister', what's the first thing that you think of? Go round the group and speak out the first thing that springs to mind. It doesn't matter if it's the same as the person before.

Then look at a short Bible story in Luke 7.36-50 – the ministry of the woman anointing the feet of Jesus.

Explain we are going to do this Bible reading with our imaginations. Ask the group to get as comfortable as possible. Then encourage the young people to imagine that they are one of the characters – it doesn't matter which one. Encourage them to think about what it feels like to be the person offering the ministry, and receiving it.

You might even find two young people from the group who are willing to have their feet washed or massaged with oil or lotion. Dramatize the reading, and ask:

- What is it like to have your feet washed?

- What is it like to wash someone's feet?

- What is it like to watch it being done?

Then write the words 'Ministry means . . .' on the flip chart, and encourage them to think of one word that summarizes what ministry is.

There are some specific ministries, but much of life is involved in ministering to others.

byte

Loads going on, but is it a ministry or just a job?

Think of your church and list the different types of ministry. How many are there? What's the difference between ministry and doing the jobs?

Then think about school, college or where you have a part-time job. How many different jobs are going on there? In what way could these be seen as ministries? For example, is washing up at the local pub just a job – how could you see it

continued >

continued >

as serving someone? What about the cleaners and teachers at college? Are they in the job just to earn a living? Is that all there is? In what way do they feel 'ministered to' by others in their everyday life? A way in to this might involve working out what they are grateful for. We don't usually appreciate our teachers, but maybe their gifts are being shared as a ministry.

Are they going to see people's work around them in a different way?

Is every job a ministry?

Ministering to each other

For this exercise, you are each going to do something kind and generous to someone else. But because ministry is an action – a doing thing – what could you do to a person, other than smiling or telling them, that would make them feel special?

- make drinks;

- massage;

- foot-washing and shoe cleaning;

- hair combing and styling;

- make something for someone;

- work out something that you would like to offer to a friend?

Then work out something you might do to minister to people in your community:

- coffee to the homeless;

- car wash ten cars;

- sweep the streets;

- shoe-shine in the town centre;

- goodie bags at the end of a service.

Live your life as if you were wearing a bumper sticker that reads: 'Practise random acts of kindness and senseless acts of beauty.'

ministries: working them out!

mega byte

Speed debating!

This may take the whole session, depending on the number of guests you have, but don't worry if it does.

Invite three or four (or more, depending on your contacts) good role models of Christians who feel that they are ministering in their occupations. These should be people from your own congregation and of any age – such as an actor, teacher, volunteer worker, minister, licensed lay minister, carer, marketing executive, school crossing attendant.

Set up as many 'stations' as you need to get one person in ministry and two or three questioners together.

Each group of questioners has five minutes to ask the person:

- What do you do most of the time?
- What do you love about what you do?
- What do you like least?
- In what way are you in ministry and living out a vocation?
- How did you know when you were being called by God?
- Has that calling or your ministry changed over time?

(If you like, have these and other questions ready on a piece of paper or from the members' handout.)

After this, you have another five minutes to go back to any of the people and find out more about their work and then receive questions.

Then gather the group together and ask:

- What have they learnt?
- What has surprised them?
- What or who has impressed them?

byte

Ministries in the news

Gather a variety of national newspapers and spot the stories where there is any kind of ministry going on (e.g. emergency services, caring professions), to illustrate the variety of ministries that underpin the way we live now.

ministries: working them out!

Wannabe

After the movement and activity of the session, it is important to end this session with some quiet and stillness. Use some quiet, ambient 'chill-out' music to act as a background (if you don't have any, ask one of the group members to bring some).

Ask the group to think silently: So what do you want to be when you grow up?

Any thoughts? Has this week changed your mind? In what way can your present desires for the future be seen as ministry?

The group doesn't need to answer these out loud, just to think about them over the next few days. End this time with a short prayer:

> **Lord,**
>
> **we thank you for all those we have met.**
>
> **Thank you for the ways you call us, for the different opportunities to serve you.**
>
> **Help us to listen to your voice whispering to us and guiding us in our next steps along the way.**
>
> **Here I am, Lord! Help me to listen. Amen.**

backing up

Ministry comes in many shapes and sizes. God will take us and use us in whatever walk of life we find ourselves provided that we allow him to use our gifts for his purposes in order to minister to the world.

ministries: working them out!

home page

To think about what it means to live out God's calling in our everyday lives and in our work.

byte

What is a ministry?

'Minister' is defined in a dictionary as a verb and means 'to serve, to attend to the needs of, to help'.

Which one word would sum up what a minister is and does?

Then look at a short Bible story in Luke 7.36-50: the ministry of the woman anointing the feet of Jesus.

There are some specific ministries, but much of life is involved in ministering to others.

byte

Loads going on!

Think of your church: list the different types of ministry. How many are there? What's the difference between ministry and doing the jobs?

warming up

Fab, sad, mad or bad!

This is a game where people have to vote on jobs and what they think of them:

What do you think of the jobs with which you come into contact day by day?

Which ones do you know about/know nothing about?

Are any of them not just jobs, but ministries?

byte

Ministering to each other

What lovely and nice thing would you like to do to someone else in the group:

- make drinks;
- massage;
- foot-washing and shoe cleaning;
- hair combing and styling;
- make something for someone
- work out something that you would like to offer to a friend;
- something else . . . . ?

Then work out something you might do to minister to people in your community:

continued >

ministries: working them out!

byte

continued >

- coffee to the homeless;
- car wash ten cars;
- sweep the streets;
- shoe-shine in the town centre;
- goodie bags at the end of a service.

Bumper sticker: 'Practise random acts of kindness and senseless acts of beauty.'

byte

Ministries in the news

Get a variety of national newspapers and spot the stories where there is a ministry, e.g. emergency services, caring professions, to illustrate the variety of ministries.

mega byte

Speed debating!

There are some guests tonight who are happy to be asked about their work and life and why they feel that they are serving God. This is your chance to quiz them!

You might want to ask these questions. You might have your own. It's up to you!

- What do you do most of the time?
- What do you love about what you do?
- What do you like least?
- In what way are you in ministry and living out a vocation?
- How did you know when you were being called by God?
- Has that calling or your ministry changed?

What else would you like to ask?

After this, you have another 5 minutes to go back to any of the people and find out more about their work and then receive questions.

interfacing

Wannabe

A reflection ending with this short prayer:

> **Lord,**
>
> **we thank you for all those we have met.**
>
> **Thank you for the ways you call us,
> for the different opportunities to serve you.**
>
> **Help us to listen to your voice whispering to us
> and guiding us in our next steps along the way.**
>
> **Here I am, Lord! Help me to listen. Amen.**

backing up

Ministry comes in many shapes and sizes. God will take us and use us in whatever walk of life we find ourselves provided that we allow him to use our gifts for his purposes in order to minister to the world.

Losing and gaining a life

You will need:
* a set of old-style balancing scales with a 'plus' and 'minus' label;
* a large number of 10p coins (estimate about 10 per group member);
* a holding cross or palm cross for each of the group members;
* a copy of the DVD of *Billy Elliot* and a DVD player.

home page

Following God's call involves both sacrifices and benefits. The aim of this session is to explore both what we stand to lose and what we stand to gain by engaging with God's purposes for us.

warming up

This warming-up activity lasts the whole session and you will need to keep bringing people back to it and reminding them (and yourself!) of it.

Display the labelled balancing scales and the pile of 10p coins. Explain to the group that, throughout the session, if they feel at any point that ministry or seeking God's call involves a sacrifice or a benefit, they can add a 10p piece to one or other of the scale pans. They can go up as many times as they like (10ps permitting!).

logging on

Thinking back to last time, what did the people we interviewed give up to fulfil their vocation? What have they gained? What has stayed with you most since last time?

byte

The call of the disciples

First explain what were the key jobs in first-century Holy Land – especially by the Sea of Galilee. Fishing was a key livelihood and without it these fishermen and their families would have been in dire straits, and yet Jesus said, 'leave your nets – I will make you fishers of people'. Then read or act out Luke 5.1-11.

What did the fishermen give up?

What would have been the hardest thing about leaving their old life to follow Jesus?

Could you imagine giving up so much and following without having any guarantees about where it was all going to end up?

What did they *not* have to give up? (Jesus still called them fishers – in other words, he still wanted them to use the gifts and skills they had, but in a different way.)

What did they gain by following Jesus' call?

Is making a sacrifice always bad? Does losing stuff make us unhappy?

Think of things you would be happy to lose:

- weight

- exams

- teacher

- homework?

Do you or they know of people who have given up a great deal to follow their dream, their instincts or where God wanted them to be?

Explain that being called and following Jesus can be scary, and we fear that we might lose so much, but the gains ultimately outweigh the losses. Following Jesus is about making sacrifices and not having everything we want, but rather having everything God wants. Many people find, though, when they follow a call from God, that what God wants becomes what they want, too.

(Don't forget to remind them to keep putting the 10ps on the scales!)

Losing and gaining a life

Billy Elliot

Watch a short clip from the film *Billy Elliot*. Go to scene 15 in the scene selection menu. (*NB Please note that this is a certificate 15 film, but the clips we have chosen are suitable for younger people*.) If your group is over 15, start the clip from scene 14. To find a synopsis of the film, if members haven't seen it, please go to www.cinema.com/film/3984/billy-elliot/synopsis.phtml

Pause the film just after the London auditions, for a discussion of some of the issues raised.

Who is making sacrifices here?

● Billy – what does he risk by pursuing his passion for dancing? (Ballet is an unusual thing for a boy to be interested in, so it might be misunderstood, and be embarrassing for him and for his family.)

● Billy's dad – what does he sacrifice, and why? (He goes against the grain by going back to work so that he can pay for travelling to the audition, and chooses to take pride in Billy even though dancing is not what he would have chosen for his son.)

● Billy's dance teacher – why is she willing to sacrifice so much of her time? (She sees that he has talent, that he will work hard, and that he's hungry to learn more.)

● Billy's older brother – how is he affected by Billy's passion for dancing? (He is torn between loyalty to his family and loyalty to his colleagues in the miners' strike.)

What enables them all to make (and then live with) their decisions? (How do they find the courage to help Billy pursue his dream even if they don't know whether he will succeed? Has anyone in the group experienced taking that kind of risk?)

At the end of the discussion show the short clip that has the results of the audition and then Billy coming in as a swan at the end of the film.

What is the result of all those sacrifices?

Is it worth it? Why?

Alternatively, you might want to take the whole session to watch the film, in which case there would be time over refreshments to discuss some of the key issues from the film about sacrifice and what this has brought the main characters. The best way to do this is to introduce the film with an outline description of the different characters as above and to ask the group to think about the sacrifices the people were making – you could even do this with the weights of 10ps on the scales!

In John's Gospel Jesus proclaims the words: 'I came so that everyone would have life, and have it in its fullest' (John 10.10, CEV).

Make the point that, after all the sacrifices, what Billy has found is his true vocation as a dancer, and in the last clip we can see that he is truly enjoying life in all its fullness, and that despite his family's sacrifices, they also share in his joy.

So what about you? What might God be calling you to?

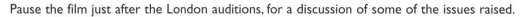

Losing and gaining a life

byte

Ten minutes to explain, one hour to give!

Making sacrifices does not necessarily mean changing the whole direction of your life as Billy Elliot did, but making a start somewhere We want to invite you to give something of your life – to make a sacrifice for one hour this week. What things might you consider giving time to? Look at the difference it might make.

How might we give an hour? What could we manage, realistically in one hour a week?

- recycling;

- visiting one person;

- praying;

- finding out about a local charity;

- walking a neighbour's dog?

interfacing

For the prayer time today, you will need small wooden holding crosses or palm crosses – one for each person.

Show some images of Christ on the cross or on his journey to the cross (perhaps three or four of the Stations of the Cross or choose some from doing an Internet image search for Jesus).

Invite the members to walk with Jesus on his way to the cross and then to sit and look at the cross and think of the sacrifice made by Jesus. 'Greater love has no one than to lay down his life for his friends.'

Losing and gaining a life

home page

The aim of this session is to explore both the sacrifices involved in ministry and following God's call, and the benefits.

warming up

This warming-up activity lasts the whole session so don't forget the scales! Every time you think that following God's call means giving something up and is a negative, then place a 10p piece on the 'minus' part of the scales. Every time you hear something that is really positive about following God, put a 10p on the 'plus' side. Keep doing this all the way through the session.

logging on

Thinking back to last time, what did the people we interviewed give up to fulfil their vocation? What have they gained? What has stayed with you most since last time?

byte

The call of the disciples

In the first-century Holy Land – especially by the Sea of Galilee – fishing was a key livelihood and without it these fishermen and their families would have been in dire straits: 'Leave your nets – I will make you fishers of people.'

Read Luke 5.1-11.

What did the disciples give up? How hard would this have been? Could you imagine giving up so much and following and not quite knowing where it was all going to end up?

Jesus still called them fishers – in other words, he still wanted them to use the gifts and skills they had but in a different way. They didn't have to give up everything.

What did they gain by following Jesus' call?

Is sacrifice always bad? Does losing stuff make us unhappy?

continued >

Losing and gaining a life

byte

continued >

Think of things you might be happy to lose:

- weight;

- exams;

- keeping your room tidy;

- helping around the home?

Do you know of people who have given up a great deal to follow their dream, their instincts or where God wanted them to be?

Being called and following Jesus can be scary, and we fear that we might lose so much, but the gains often outweigh the losses. Following Jesus is about making sacrifices and not having everything we want, but rather having everything that God wants.

mega byte

Billy Elliot

In the film *Billy Elliot*, who is making sacrifices?

- Billy – what does he risk by pursuing his passion for dancing?

- Billy's dad – what does he sacrifice, and why?

- Billy's dance teacher – why is she willing to sacrifice so much of her time?

- Billy's older brother – how is he affected by Billy's passion for dancing?

What enables them all to make (and then live with) their decisions?

In John's Gospel Jesus proclaims the words: 'I came so that everyone would have life, and have it in its fullest' (John 10.10, CEV). How do we see Billy 'living life to the full' in the film?

So what about you? What might God be calling you to?

Losing and gaining a life

byte

Ten minutes to explain, one hour to give!

Give up an hour this week!

How might we give an hour? What could we manage, realistically in one hour a week?

- recycling;

- visiting one person;

- praying;

- finding out about a local charity;

- walking a neighbour's dog?

interfacing

Hold the cross in your hand and focus on the images of Jesus.

Walk with Jesus on his way to the cross and then sit and look at the cross and think of the sacrifice made by Jesus. 'Greater love has no one than to lay down his life for his friends.'

NB This can be taken at any time over the 5-week period but needs to be before the final session

This session is not a formal gathering of the group, but an opportunity for group members on their own to work alongside a Christian in the local community who is fulfilling his or her vocation at work.

As outlined in Session 1, we hope that each group member has by now arranged some level of work 'shadowing' and has some questions to ask.

More details for both those in work and the group members shadowing are in the resource sheets on pp. 43–44.

We have added in this session because the best way to learn is Jesus' model of apprentice and disciple. Jesus taught and showed his disciples, but he then wanted them to engage in his ministry alongside him, after which they reflected on this and learned from it. It is a model used in training and work practices in many different professions today. While we can talk for ages about God's call, we want the group to see this call in action.

Your role as leaders in this session is simply to ensure that each group member has someone to shadow, to liaise with that person and give them a clear brief on what is expected (see Resource sheet 1 on p. 43).

After the work shadow, please don't forget to write and thank all those who have taken part.

We encourage you not to go on to Session 5 until everyone has completed their short work shadowing.

Becoming me: action reflection time

You will need:

* flip chart and pens;
* smaller pieces of paper/stickers for the warming-up exercise;
* a box on which to stand;
* some stones (larger pieces of gravel or pebbles from a beach are fine) and a bowl of water;
* one small mirror or mirror tile for each member of the group;
* individual group members' notes from their work-shadowing placements;
* some smaller pieces of paper, and pens/pencils for writing and drawing.

home page

This session is an opportunity for the group to reflect together on their experiences of work shadowing and interviewing Christians in real jobs in the placement that they will have undertaken at some point during the last few weeks. It also looks to the future, and how we can make some of the biggest decisions of our lives in the light of our desire to live God's way.

warming up

Who am I?

Each member of the group needs to have a piece of paper taped to their back (or a sticker stuck to their forehead) upon which is written the name of a famous person.
They must find out who they are by asking 'yes' or 'no' questions of the other members of the group. Are they pleased or disappointed with who they turned out to be?

logging on

Explain that the group members' experiences of work shadowing and interviewing Christians in real jobs in the placement that they will have undertaken at some point during the last few weeks has given them an opportunity to reflect on the reality of living out our Christian discipleship in the real world. In the light of this, today's session will also look to the future, and how we can make some of the biggest decisions of our lives in the light of our desire to live God's way.

Becoming me: action reflection time

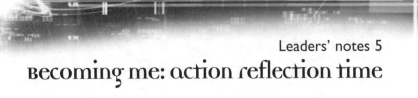

byte

The fourth plinth

In Trafalgar Square there is an empty pedestal (the 'fourth plinth', see **www.fourthplinth.co.uk**) upon which every so often a new statue or other sculpture is placed. Give some background to the history of the four plinths, and the military and other heroes of the time who are permanently displayed on the other three plinths. Each one of the heroes is there because their contribution to this country has been recognized and celebrated and is there for all to see. Ask the group to consider what or who they would want to put on the fourth plinth: what statement would they want to make to all who would see it? The idea is to try to express what they think is most important to them. Invite each person to devise something that communicates what they think their 'gift' to the world should be. They can draw their image on the flip chart, or they could 'act' it out themselves, standing on the box.

mega byte

God at work?

Spend a few minutes in small groups, asking the group members to share their experiences of work shadowing.

- Was the job what they expected? Did anything surprise them?

- What did they learn about what it is like for Christians in the workplace?

- Did anyone gain an insight into their own possible career plans as a result of the placement?

Invite the groups to share some of their discussion with the whole group.

You might like to watch the DVD resource 'transforming lives' (available to download from **www.transforminglives.org.uk**) – a series of sound bites from Christians who are working in the teaching profession – as a way in to thinking about what difference Christian faith makes in the world of work.

вєсомιng mє: αςτιση ρєflєςτιση τιmє

byte

What will we be?

- Look back: how have you changed since week one?

- What part can God play in your choices, now and in the future?

Ask each member of the group to draw a simple graph or picture of their life in the future, with two lines on it, one for 'my plan' and one for 'God's plan'.

- What key events, situations, people, hopes, fears, and dreams can you show on the plan?

- How do the two lines overlap and interact with each other?

- How do we keep on working out what God wants us to do?

- What is your ambition? What is God's ambition?

byte

Living life to the full

In John 10.10 (CEV), Jesus says 'I came so that everyone would have life, and have it in its fullest.'

St Irenaeus of Lyons (c. 130–200) said that 'the glory of God is a human being fully alive'.

- Discuss in small groups, or draw a picture, of how life in all its fullness might look (for you).

    now;

    in three years' time;

    in the long-term future.

- How can God's glory be shown in our lives?

    in our current situation at home, at school/college, in the community;

    by what we will do for a living;

    by the way we spend our time, our energy, our money;

    simply by being who we are?

- What makes you feel 'fully alive'?

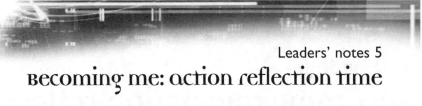

Becoming me: action reflection time

byte

Finding myself

In pairs or small groups, look at the quotations/testimonies on the supplementary handout. Does anything strike a chord?

Now look at the three pairs of statements about vocation at the end of that handout. For each pair of statements, think about which of the pair relates more to your own experience and ideas about vocation, and why.

interfacing

Being myself

Place a heap of stones and the bowl of water in the centre of the circle, and invite each member of the group to take a stone, look at it, and hold it in their hands, considering its rough edges, its brokenness, its colour, size and shape, its uniqueness.

Then invite those in the group who wish to do so to bring their stone forward and drop it into the bowl, observing the ripples created on the surface of the water. The stones represent ourselves: all that we have to offer, our gifts, and our past experiences and the way they have affected us. The bowl of water is the world, and the ripples are the way in which we affect and contribute to the world when we offer ourselves in God's service.

Now, give each person in the group a small mirror or mirror tile and ask them to spend a few moments just looking at their own reflection. Then read the meditation on the members' handout, and end with the prayer outline on the handout, inviting members of the group to fill in the gaps, gathering all the strands of the weeks together in a simple act of dedication.

backing up

Vocation is different for everyone because we are all unique. Each of us is called by God to become who he created us to be. We each have something to offer to the world through our work, and the whole of our lives.

Becoming me: action reflection time

home page

What did you learn from your experiences of work shadowing and interviewing a Christian in a real job? And what can you take from these last few weeks as you look forward to the future? How will you make some of the biggest decisions of your life in the light of your desire to live God's way?

byte

The fourth plinth

In Trafalgar Square there is an empty pedestal (the 'fourth plinth', see **www.fourthplinth.co.uk**) upon which every so often a new statue or other work of art is placed. What would you put on the plinth for all to see?

Becoming me: action reflection time

mega byte

God at work?

Think about your experiences of work shadowing.

- Was the job what you expected? Did anything surprise you?

- What did you learn about what it is like for Christians in the workplace?

- Did you gain an insight into your own possible career plans?

- Look back: how have you changed since week one?

- What part will God play in your choices, now and in the future?

byte

What will I be?

Draw a simple graph or picture of your life in the future, with two lines on it, one for 'my plan' and one for 'God's plan'.

- What key events, situations, people, hopes, fears and dreams can you show on the plan?

- How do the two lines overlap and interact with each other?

- How do we keep on working out what God wants us to do?

- What is your ambition? What is God's ambition?

byte

Living life to the full

In John 10.10 (CEV), Jesus says 'I came so that everyone would have life, and have it in its fullest.'

St Irenaeus of Lyons (c. 130–200) said that 'the glory of God is a human being fully alive'.

continued >

Becoming me: action reflection time

byte

continued >

- How might life in all its fullness look:

    now?

    in three years' time?

    in the long-term future?

- How can God's glory be revealed in our lives?

    in our current situation at home, at school/college, in the community;

    by what we will do for a living;

    by the way we spend our time, our energy, our money;

    simply by being who we are?

- What makes you feel 'fully alive'?

interfacing

Being myself

We each bring ourselves, our past, our gifts, and our experiences. If we offer them to God, we can make a huge difference to the world. What will you offer God today?

A meditation

Everything I look at shouts back at me telling me to change:

Be like this

Wear that

Change your life

Have a makeover

You are what you eat.

Everything I look at shouts at me telling me to become someone else

But I can't!

continued >

Becoming me: action reflection time

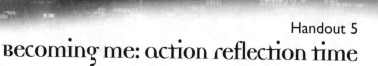

interfacing

continued >

A label is only a label

Food is just food.

I look in the mirror and want to change how I am because of all that.

I am not good enough.

I look in the mirror and because of all those voices I don't like what I see.

Someone I read about whispers back at me not to change:

'Be yourself

I will clothe you

I will be the change in your life

I made you, you don't need making over!

Feed on me.'

Someone I read about whispers back at me to just be me!

How can I?

With all those voices – I can hardly hear the whisper I want to hear.

I look in the mirror and still want to change.

Surely I am not good enough.

I look in the mirror, and someone looks back at me and says:

'I love what I see because I made you and formed you

Before you were born, millions of cells multiplied into you

Hand crafted into what you see now and what I see now.

You are one in a million

You are unique

Utterly loved without condition, without expectation,

Just the longing that you will love me in return

And be you!'

continued >

Becoming me: action reflection time

interfacing

continued >

Final prayer

Loving Lord,

thank you for calling me in my baptism.

Thank you for my gifts in . . .

I pray for all those who are serving you in different ways and ministries, especially . . .

I offer myself to you afresh

and pray that you would help me to hear you calling me,

and help me to follow you.

Amen.

processing

- What do you believe to be the purpose that God has for your life? How can you find out?

- What is the thing that is uniquely yours to offer to the world in the service of God?

do something about it

If you have an idea of the sort of work you might want to do in the future, try to find someone who is doing that job, and talk to them, and perhaps organize another (longer) work-shadowing placement.

If you can think of an adult Christian that you really admire, ask to speak to them about their experiences of their work, how they made their choices of career and life, and how their faith and their working life connect.

becoming me: action reflection time

Finding myself byte: experiences of living out God's call

I love food. I've always loved food, and being on *Masterchef* is giving me a unique opportunity to bring all my enthusiasm, passion, and creativity together. If I win I will want to share my passion with as many people as possible by opening my own restaurant.

Contestant on BBC 2's Masterchef Goes Large, *2005*

I believe that my life has been shaped into a bowl and that all these wonderful opportunities that have come my way are gifts from God, to grow and ripen, like pieces of fruit. As I continue on my fruitful journey I know that I am growing into the person that God wants me to be.

Trainee pastoral assistant

I always thought that going into teaching would mean that I had to stop doing all the other things I'd enjoyed doing before, but actually I use my gifts in art and music all the time – it's as if now I'm doing what I'm meant to be doing with my life, I'm finally using 'all of me', not just 'part of me'.

A newly qualified teacher

Since I started thinking about ministry, I've felt more and more fully myself, more and more alive. Despite the struggles that working full time in ministry brings, I have never felt more fulfilled than I do now.

A parish priest

Finding my vocation was like gradually starting to see in colour instead of in black and white. Now this is what I do all the time, and every day the colours get richer and stronger.

An artist

Sometimes I hate my job, but I'm actually pretty good at it, and even when it's boring or frustrating for me, I know that I'm making a difference to people and making their lives that little bit less frustrating – in a sense, that's job satisfaction, and I suppose that's also ministry!

A computer help desk employee

God's gift has always been my piano playing. Even though I spent years working for a big high street chain, and God helped me to do that, now I feel I want to use those God-given gifts for the rest of my life. I want to teach piano, I feel this is not a job, it's my calling.

A Christian making a career change

Becoming me: action reflection time

Vocation means . . .

My job ←————————————————→ **My life**

Making sacrifices ←————————————→ **Gaining benefits**

What God wants ←————————————→ **What I want**

Draw a cross on each line to show where you are in your thinking about vocation.
You could look at this again in six months' time and see if you've moved!

role modelling

Notes for those offering placements

Thank you for offering a work-shadowing experience to .... (name).

These notes are to help you prepare for the placement, and to help the young person placed with you to get the most out of his or her experience.

- Be as honest as you can about your job:

  what does your work involve?

  how did you come to be doing your job?

  what are the best and worst aspects of your work?

- Be prepared to talk about how your faith affects you in your working life:

  did your faith play a part in your choice of career?

  have there been times when your faith has helped you at work?

  has your work and your faith ever seemed to pull you in different directions?

- What about your life generally?

  how do you find a healthy balance between work, family, rest, God, leisure, etc?

  do you feel that you have had to sacrifice or give anything up to live the life you live now?

  what or who was most helpful when you were thinking about what to do with your life?

role modelling

Notes for those undertaking placements

My role modelling placement was with:

Name..

Date..

Job ....

What struck you about the job itself?

And about the career path and choices that led to it?

What did you feel were the best and worst aspects of the job?

What surprised you most?

Can Christian faith play a part in career choices?

What difference does faith in God make to the way we go about our working lives or our studies?

When might faith conflict with what is expected of us at work?

What would be a healthy balance between work, family, rest, God, leisure?

What sacrifices might we have to make if we are to follow God's plan for our working lives?

What would you like to find out more about?

Notes to guests 'speed debating'

Thank you for being willing to take part in this session.

You have been invited to take part in speed debating! The purpose of this session is to help the young people find out more about the different jobs that people do but more importantly how these can be seen as God using our gifts and talents in different areas of work.

The group members will have only a few minutes to ask you lots of questions so please keep your answers clear and concise. Please be as open and as honest as you can be. The group has set up ground rules and, this far in to the sessions, the group should have developed a mutual respect and trust so will not disclose specifics of what you have said. What you share with individuals remains with them. Please be open about your faith and the part it plays in your work – how it guides you and informs you, but also the struggles of living as a Christian in your particular field of work.

You will be asked to remain in one place where the group meets and different members of the group will come to you. After a few minutes, and on the signal of the leader, the young people will move on to the next person and another one will come to you with the same or similar questions.

The leaders are duty bound to ensure that you have been through a CRB records check before the session.

You are not here to ask questions of the young people, but simply to help them find out more about you and your work. This is not an interview, but much more of a rapid fire *Question Time*.

Enjoy!

Appendix 1: worship

Getting young people to work together on preparing a youth service on the theme of vocation, or a presentation during a mainstream service, can be a good way of following up on many of the themes explored in this resource.

- If the group has never planned worship before, invite them to brainstorm what the essential elements are in a worship service. They may come up with ideas including:

  gathering;

  hearing God in the Bible, whether through reading or drama;

  prayer, which might be led from the front, participatory, multi-sensory;

  praise and worship, e.g. singing songs or hymns, or listening to a band leading worship;

  teaching or reflection, on the theme or Bible passage;

  response to God, which might be verbal, creative, sacramental;

  being sent out, changed by encounter with God.

Then set about reinterpreting these elements in their own style.

Ideally someone who is experienced at planning worship should help facilitate this.

- Using drama:

One youth group wrote and produced a short drama entitled 'deal or no deal?' based on the popular TV quiz, but with the boxes containing different job titles, of varying 'status'. Using drama can be a good way of affirming the dramatic and literary gifts of group members, while those who are stage-shy can have responsibility for creating props, lighting and sound effects, and stage management.

- Prayer and reflection:

'Multisensory suggestions include, placing pebbles in a bowl of water (the stones are all different colours, shapes and sizes and textures, to reflect ourselves, and how we are broken, chipped, beautiful, etc.). A similar exercise uses bricks (preferably old and worn, with mortar still stuck to them) that can be used to build a wall or tower. Prayers could be written on 'graffiti sheets' pinned to the walls, rather than being spoken.

- Using music:

Many of the standard hymns and songs on the theme of vocation are well known, at least in some churches, or are easily learned (for example, 'I, the Lord of sea and sky', and 'Will you come and follow me?'). While some youth groups like to sing, others prefer to listen. Can any group members suggest contemporary popular music tracks that explore self-identity, work–life balance, or any other relevant themes?

- Remember practical things such as whether there will be an order of service and who will produce it; whether microphones are available and who will need to use them; and any other logistical issues associated with the venue.

- Remember to advertise the service in local schools and colleges; anywhere where young people gather, and to the rest of the church congregation(s) with which the group is associated.

Appendix 2: further reading and resources

Bible stories suitable for further study and reflection

Personal calling stories

The call of Abraham	Genesis 12.1-3
The call of Samuel	1 Samuel 3.1-10
The call of Isaiah	Isaiah 6.1-8
The call of the first disciples	Matthew 4.18-19; Mark 1.16-20; Luke 5.1-11; John 1.35-42

Calls to belong

Being children of God	Matthew 5.9; 1 John 3.1
The body and its members	1 Corinthians 12.12-26
The Early Church	Acts 2.44-47

Gifts and talents

The gifts of the Spirit	Romans 12.4-8; 1 Corinthians 12.4-11
The parable of the talents	Matthew 25.14-30
Our gifts are from God	1 Peter 4.10-11

Hard callings

The call of Jonah	Jonah (all of it)
Paul wrestles with himself	Romans 7.15-25
The cost of discipleship	Matthew 8.18-22; Mark 8.34-38; Luke 14.26-33

Work and life

Working as if for God	Colossians 3.23
Mary and Martha	Luke 10.38-42
What's worth working for?	John 6.27-29
Tilling the land	Genesis 2.15

Being sent out

The great commission	Matthew 28.16-20
Jesus' own calling	Luke 4.16-21

Books

J. Baker, *Life Actually*, Scripture Union, 2005 (a short book on life choices for those in Year 11)

C. Bartlam, *Mind the Gap*, Scripture Union, 1999 (a short book on gap year experiences)

R. Hall-Smith, *On-line with God: Careers advice with Almightly input*, Kevin Mayhew, 2004 (options at 16 and 18)

Poems

E. Gateley, 'Called to become', *Psalms of a Laywoman*, Sheed and Ward, 1999

J. Powell, 'You have a special message to deliver', *Through Seasons of the Heart*, Thomas More Association, 1996

Periodicals

Youth Work, December 2006, on the calling of youth work and workers

Films

Billy Elliot, Universal, 2000 – discovering a gift; making sacrifices to pursue it; the importance of other people in helping us fulfil our potential

The Lord of the Rings trilogy, New Line Cinema, 2001–2003 – vocation isn't just for the 'usual suspects' but people who seem weak or insignificant can be called too; power can be abused as well as used

Dead poets society, Touchstone, 1989 – gifts are not always understood; the cost of not being able to follow a calling

Pay it forward, Warner, 2001 – we each have something important to do in the world – each person can make a difference

Music

Recommending too much music is not helpful since trends change so much, and we suggest that group members might have some of their own music to contribute – live if you have some musicians. But the following are good at creating a conducive and relaxed environment for worship. Much of this can be downloaded cheaply from the Internet.

Karl Jenkins, *Adiemus* and *Mass for the armed man*

Einaudi, *Una mattina*

Film score music from *The Mission* (Ennio Morricone) and *Atonement*

Various, *Classical Chillout*

Plainsong, *various CDs available.*